A   GIFT   FOR   MY   FRIEND

F R O M

----

*(Look for other personal notes in this book
on pages 33 and 89.)*

a good friend
refreshes the soul

Lemonade
in the Desert

LES & LESLIE
PARROTT

COUNTRYMAN
®

NASHVILLE, TENNESSEE

The greatest sweetener of human life is Friendship. To raise this to the highest pitch of enjoyment, is a secret which but few discover.

—Joseph Addison

Contents

Introduction

Good friends. Over the years, they have comforted you, irked you and, more than a few times, saved your skin. They are the friends you have known for years but still can't wait to see next week for lunch. Loyal and lasting, these friends stand by you in good and bad, like a pair of boots that have worn well. You wouldn't trade them for anything—and if you didn't have them, you'd trade almost everything to get them. The world is a wilderness without good friends.

The young Persian soldier must have felt this acutely when he was asked by his king, Cyrus the Great, whether he would trade the horse on which he had just won a race for an entire kingdom. "Certainly not, Sire," the young soldier replied, "but I would gladly part with him to gain a good friend, if I could find anyone worthy of such fellowship."

Good friends can be hard to find. Acquaintances, associates, partners, and colleagues are found in abundance. Even a friend of the fair-weather variety is not uncommon. But a good friend—the kind who makes time, keeps a secret, and forgives faults—is as scarce as lemonade in the desert.

And information about friendship is almost as rare as friends themselves. During the past few decades, we have seen an inexhaustible supply of studies on marriage and family relationships. Yet the relationship between two good friends has hardly been touched. A study at the University of Hartford looked at scores of articles in popular magazines and found fourteen articles on marriage and family relationships for every one article on friendship. "Our culture is obsessed with romance," the researchers concluded. "Friendship is seen as secondary; no one thinks it has to be talked about."

But it should be. Every autumn on our university campus, we teach a unique course dedicated to building better relationships—especially with friends. We talk a lot about friendship. And we begin by posing a simple question to our students: What makes a good friend?

Over the years we have seen responses to this question from hundreds of students, plus thousands of seminar participants. And the results have become almost predictable. In fact, this book is a summary of the top eight traits people say are the most important for being a good friend. Each chapter is our attempt to write to "the heart of this matter" by amplifying these qualities and exploring how we can make them a part of the friendships that matter most.

Les and Leslie Parrott
Center for Relationship Development
Seattle Pacific University

CHAPTER 1

A Good Friend Makes Time

A friend to all is a friend to none.

—English Proverb

It was 9:00 on a Thursday evening and the second leg of my flight had been canceled. I was stuck in the Denver Airport and wondering how I would make it to my speaking engagement late that night. I couldn't get through to the conference coordinators, so I called a friend who lived nearby: "Barb, you won't believe where I am . . ." Two minutes later, she and her husband were on their way to pick me up.

My friend Lucy would have done the same thing. On more than one occasion she has whisked through our front door, arms loaded down with bags of gourmet groceries. "I'm not going to stay," she will say, "I just want to drop off a few things for your dinner tonight." When I'm sick or simply tired, she seems to have a sixth sense when it comes to helping out at just the right time.

So does Monty. We had just finished speaking to a group of students at a retreat center in Kentucky when we returned to our room and heard a loud knock at our door. "Monty Lobb?!" Leslie exclaimed. We couldn't believe it. Monty had driven four hours —one way—from Cincinnati and tracked us down

God gives us our relatives—
thank God we can choose our friends.

—Ethel Watts Mumford

without an address. "I knew I could find you," he said with a big bear hug. "I heard you were near Wilmore and I just had to see you." We talked and laughed for about an hour and a half, then Monty drove drive home, another four hours on the road before teaching Sunday school the next morning at his church.

Few actions speak more loudly about the value of a good friend than making time. After all, friendships today are in a cancerous state—undernourished, withering, dying—because few people make the time required to keep them alive. Friends forget to phone, fail to write, ignore important events, stand each other up, and let each other down. Some gloss over the fate of a friendship and blame its demise on busy schedules, pressing deadlines, or geographical distance. But we all know that most failing friendships suffer from only one ailment: neglect.

It's no wonder that "making time" ranks high on the list of what matters most in a good friend. We juggle so many things, it's easy for friendship to take a back seat. But here's news that will encourage you to put friends back at the top of your priority list. A growing body of research says ignoring friendship not only diminishes your quality of life but could also be a health hazard. Close friendships act as an ounce of prevention, bolstering the immune system and reducing the risk of illnesses like colds, flu and perhaps even heart disease and other serious disorders. That makes maintaining friendships a health must, right up there with exercising and eating right.

In a landmark study at the University of Michigan, researchers analyzed all the relevant evidence they could find and discovered that people with strong ties to family and friends had a significantly longer average life span than those who did not. Researchers reached the startling conclusion that the lack of supportive relationships is as dangerous as well-known risks such as smoking, high blood pressure or obesity.

Quite simply, research is saying that you need to do what you want to do: Make time for friends. And never let yourself feel guilty about it. We too often equate spending time with our friends as frivolous, a sign of being lazy. That's nonsense. Making time is a noble calling for kindred spirits. It refers to the

> *Often we have no time for our friends but all the time in the world for our enemies.*
> —Leon Uris

ability of two people to influence and shape each other's lives by changing plans, thoughts, actions, and emotions. Making time means getting off work early to accompany a friend to an anxiety-provoking doctor's appointment. It means canceling a commitment to attend a friend's recital.

Six hours after Sarah's baby was born, her doctor gave her a pass to leave the hospital so she could serve as matron of honor at her friend Jean's wedding. "I showed up ten minutes before the ceremony and she was so surprised she cried and cried. Afterward Jean and her husband stopped by the hospital, still in their formal wedding wear, so they could see the baby before they left on their honeymoon." Good friends make time for each other.

We all know that good friends make time in significant life events or moments of crisis—when a friend's emotional bottoming out, for example, means canceling another commitment to provide a shoulder of support. After all, that's what friends are for. But making time in the midst of the mundane is of equal value. For some, it may require scheduling an intimate compress of information a couple of times a month. Others may need more spontaneity. Whatever the schedule, making time is what keeps a good friendship from floundering.

Remember when we were kids? The hours spent with friends were too numerous to count. But contemporary life as adults, with its tight schedules and crowded appointment books, has forced most friendships into something requiring intention and pursuit just to keep it going. Let's be honest. Making time for friends means sacrifice. But this sacrifice will counter–attack the urgency of life and create a space for one of the things that matter most in this life: friends.

A Good Friend
Keeps a Secret

Lemonade in the Desert

It is more shameful to distrust one's friends than to be deceived by them.

—Francois, Duc de La Rochefoucauld

I recently saw an advertisement dominated by a drawing of a nineteenth-century rabbi, the Chofetz Chaim, who wrote a book about gossip called Guard Your Tongue. At the bottom of the ad was a "hotline" number to call if you have information about a friend's potential marriage, business partner, or whatever. A rabbi at the other end tells you whether your gossip is important enough to pass along. If not, you are counseled to guard your tongue.

Interesting, isn't it? The advertisement reveals as much about the state of our friendships as it does

A gossip betrays a confidence, but a trustworthy man keeps a secret.

—Proverbs 11:13, NIV

about our propensity for gossip. Who among us hasn't been hurt by a broken confidence? It usually begins when your friend says to someone: "You have to promise you won't tell Brenda I told you this because she made me swear not to tell anyone . . ." It sounds very confidential. But then why are they telling you the secret? Your friend appears to be keeping a secret but isn't. Jesus understood this when He said, "Therefore, whatever you have spoken in the dark will be heard in the light, and what you have spoken in the ear in inner rooms will be proclaimed on the housetops" (Luke 12:3).

We've all shared private and personal information with a trusted friend only to learn later that our friend has blabbed it to the world. But can we still expect a friend to keep their mouth closed. Yes . . . if they're a good friend. We need to tell our secrets. Sharing helps us explore what's troubling us and sometimes leads to helpful feedback. It lets us test the reaction to what we've been holding in our heart. Not only that, it's a relief knowing we're not the only person who has experienced a certain temptation or tragedy. We feel less alone when we unburden our soul and a friend says "me too" or "I understand." Sharing a secret with a trustworthy friend can bring us closer together and deepen our relationship.

But if we expect our secret to stay secret, we need a friend we can trust. A friend who considers it a true privilege to hear what's on our mind and leave it at that. We need a human vault.

Finding a trusted friend begins by understanding why some friends are not so predisposed to keep a confidence. There are a number of reasons.

One reason is that some don't see the harm in revealing a little information. "I find that when I am gossiping about my friends, as well as my enemies, I am deeply conscious of performing a social duty," notes anthropologist Max Gluckman with tongue in cheek. "But when I hear they gossip about me, I am rightfully filled with righteous indignation."

The need to be "in the know," to have the inside scoop, is another powerful motivator for friends to unseal their lips. After all, everyone enjoys knowing information that most people aren't privy to. Experts who have studied gossip believe we all indulge in a little gossip from time to time because talking about others is a part of our behavioral makeup, ingrained in us both socially and psychologically. "If a group of friends are engaged in a gabfest, you naturally want to join in," says Dr. Jack Levin, a sociology professor at Northeastern University and author of Gossip: The Inside Scoop. That need to feel accepted encourages the gossip at times to embellish stories about people. If he is included in the conversation, he knows the group is accepting him, and to be included in the conversation he has to have something interesting to say. In a university experiment conducted by Professor Levin, gossip about a campus wedding was spread among the student body of a large university. The wedding was fictitious, it never happened, yet twelve percent of the students questioned said they had attended the wedding. Some of them even went so far as to describe the wedding gown.

There are countless reasons beyond ignorance and social acceptance that a friend might blab your secret. But whatever the cause, there is no disputing the fact that gossip always causes pain. Rumors travel like the wind, intensifying as they circulate. Cheap prattle, particularly that preceded by "don't tell a soul," takes on a

> *Gossip separates close friends.*
> —**Proverbs 16:28, NIV**

life of its own, disintegrating a friendship in moments what has taken years to build. That's why a good friend keeps a secret. Oh the comfort of feeling safe with a friend, having neither to edit thoughts nor weigh words!

We all want this kind of a friend, but we do well remember that we must also be this kind of friend.

For most of her life, Kathie Lee Gifford has followed the same morning ritual. Before breakfast, before her feet even touch the floor, she prays: "Lord, please help me today. Don't let me hurt anyone with my mouth." She writes about it in her autobiography, *I Can't Believe I Said That!* I wonder if the apostle Paul said the same thing. He certainly warned about the condemnation that comes to "gossips and busy bodies" who say "things which they ought not" (1

> *None are so fond of secrets as those who do not mean to keep them.*
>
> —Charles Caleb Colton

Timothy 5:13). Truth is, we've all been victims of a friend's loose lips. And we've all hurt friends by

Lemonade in the Desert

not keeping quiet. That's why a good friend also forgives faults.

Neither a friend nor ourselves can "unspeak" a rumor, anymore than we can snatch back a bullet we have just fired. Once out, it is gone. But ultimately, there is One in whom we can always find safety, one who is supremely trustworthy. Even though we might not always understand God's ways, we can share our deepest secrets with Him in full confidence. David wrote about it in Psalm 62:5–8:

"My soul, wait silently for God alone,

For my expectation is from Him.

He only is my rock and my salvation;

He is my defense;

I shall not be moved. . . .

Trust in Him at all times, you people;

Pour out your heart before Him;

God is a refuge for us."

A Good Friend
Cares Deeply

Lemonade in the Desert

To the query, "What is a friend?" his reply was "A single soul dwelling in two bodies."
—Aristotle

Tina came to my office on a crisp autumn morning, steaming latte in hand, and slunk into a cozy chair in the corner. We had been meeting together for four or five weeks of relationship counseling when we started exploring the issue of friendship. Tina told me she had a relational loose end with a friend she'd known since grade school. Turns out they hadn't spoken in more than a year but Tina didn't know why.

"Was there some kind of betrayal or rift?" I asked.

"Not really," Tina replied. "At least not that I can remember."

"Well then, what was it?

Tina thought for a moment, shrugged her shoulders, then confessed: "I guess I just stopped caring."

Enough said. Once you remove care from friendship, its over. There's nothing left to discuss. It's like removing blood from the body. Friendship cannot survive without care.

Care is so germane, so essential to the relationship that it often goes unnoticed. Ask people what matters most in a good friend and they might not list care. But when you put this quality on a list of traits and ask people to rate its importance, you'll see it near the top. Why? Because without care friendship is impossible. Three little words—"I don't care"—are a deadly bullet in the heart of friendship.

Frank Reed may understand the value of caring as well as anyone I know of. From 1986 to 1990, he was held hostage in Lebanon. He was blindfolded for months at a time, living in complete darkness. He was chained to a wall and kept in absolute silence. On one occasion, Reed was moved to another cell, and, although blindfolded, he could sense others in

Goodness consists not in the outward things we do but in the inward things we are.

—Edwin Hubbel Chapin

the room. Only weeks later did he learn he was chained next to fellow American hostages Terry Anderson and Tom Sutherland.

In his years as a prisoner, Reed was humiliated,

beaten, made ill, and tormented. But Reed's worst pain was not knowing if anyone cared. In an interview with Time, Reed said "Nothing I did mattered to anyone. I began to realize how withering it is to exist with not a single expression of caring around [me] . . . I learned one overriding fact: caring is a powerful force. If no one cares, you are truly alone."

It seems funny that we toss this vital force around so (forgive me) carelessly. "Take care" we say to the grocery clerk who rings up our items. "Take care," we say at the

> *You're blessed when you care. At the moment of being "care-full," you find yourselves cared for.*
>
> —Matthew 5: 7
> (The Message)

end of a phone conversation with a near stranger. But when was the last time you took time to consider what "taking care" really means?

The word "care" comes the Germanic kar, which originally meant "sad." It alludes to the idea that a caring person feels sad when you feel sad. Care is a kind of compassion that allows a friend to enter your world and feel your pain. Care says that whatever happens to you happens to me, when sadness hits you it hits me, too. Of course, care also says that when something terrific happens to you I rejoice myself. Your life makes a genuine difference to my own life. That's the essence of caring deeply.

When we truly care for a friend—at a deep and meaningful level—we involve both our heart and our head. We think our friend's thoughts and feel our friend's emotions. When we care for a friend, we pay close attention to their experience. We listen and watch for ways to be helpful. We take notice and attend to their world as if it were our own. It's what Aristotle meant when he said a friend is "a single soul dwelling in two bodies."

You don't have to be a hostage to appreciate the power of care. All of us practice caring instinctively. Like handling a crystal vase, we're careful with things we value. But a good friend cultivates care at a deep level, never taking it for granted.

A Note to My Friend

.... ,

Thank you for the ways you show how much you care.

I especially appreciate . . .

....

....

....

....

....

....

....

....

A Good Friend Provides Space

By myself I am not large enough to call the whole person into activity; I want other lights than my own to show all his facets. Hence true friendship is the least jealous of loves.
—C. S. Lewis

Jeff was one of my best friends in college—for about six weeks. We met at a student orientation meeting. All afternoon we listened to talks about campus protocol, study tips, and proper procedures. That evening we ended up together in the dining hall. I was passing on the traditional hot meal choices and headed straight to the cereal bar for a heaping bowl of corn flakes. That's when I noticed Jeff right on my heels.

"You like cereal for dinner, too?" Jeff asked.

"Not really, I'm not that hungry tonight."

"I can't believe you like corn flakes with a banana on it," Jeff exclaimed. "That's exactly what I like."

As we placed our twin trays on the same table and sat down to eat, I was amazed by all the things we readily had in common. It turned out that all the classes I was enrolled in, Jeff was signed up to take as well. We lived on different floors of the same residence hall, but he was petitioning to move to the very same floor I was on. He planned to work out in the gym during the same time of day as me. It was

I don't like to talk much with people who always agree with me. It is amusing to coquette with an echo for a little while, but one soon tires of it.

—Thomas Carlyle

uncanny, the list went on and on. We shopped at the same stores for our clothes. We both liked mint chip ice cream. I'd never met anyone with whom I'd had more in common.

As the days rolled by, Jeff and I were developing a close and comfortable friendship. It seemed almost effortless. We talked freely and frequently. Never had a cross word, or a differing opinion for that matter. We eat our meals together. Studied in the library. Hung out on the weekends. We were close—and that was the problem.

My fast friendship with Jeff eventually made me feel uneasy. Jeff, I learned, wasn't scheduled to be in the same classes as me until he discovered what classes I was taking. He hadn't planned to move to the same floor as me until he learned were I was living. Jeff probably didn't even like corn flakes. Our pseudo sameness revealed itself after an encounter in the campus dining hall. On this particular night I decided to eat dinner with some guys from my floor. Half way through our meal, Jeff showed up in a huff.

"Thanks for waiting for me," Jeff sneered as he passed our table.

"What's that about?" asked one of the guys at the table.

"You got me," I said with genuine confusion.

I didn't give it more than a moment's thought until later that evening when I encountered Jeff at the library.

"You could at least say you're sorry," Jeff said before I uttered a word.

"I don't know what you're talking about," I responded.

Jeff proceeded to tell me that I was insensitive because I went to dinner without him. What's more, he told me that the date I had scheduled with my girlfriend that weekend was "uncool" because he thought we were going to the basketball game together. Around this time I also began noticing he questioned me about anything and everything. "Who was that on the phone?" "What time do you think you'll be home from your date?" "Are you going to study with me tonight?" I started to wonder whether Jeff had become my mother inside the skin of a freshman college student. I half expected him to ask me what I was going to be wearing the next day so our clothes would coordinate.

My friendship with Jeff faded as quickly as it began. We were off to a pretty good start, I thought, but being smothered gets old fast. No matter how close the connection, sometimes we all need room to

I cannot give you the formula for success, but I can give you the formula for failure: Try to please everybody.

—Herbert Bayard Swope

breathe. I suppose that's why so many people say a good friend provides space. Without space, our relationships wither—the consuming friend leaves us gasping for air, longing for a fresh breeze.

Overly engaged and emotionally needy friends who don't give you space are like a relentless heat-wave. The warmth feels nice at first, but it eventually wears you down, depletes you of energy. This kind of friend mothers and smothers you with their very presence. Their constant connecting becomes oppressive—if not possessive. This kind of friend has no appreciation for what C. S. Lewis meant when he

There is no conversation more boring than the one where everybody agrees.
—Michel de Montaigne

said: "In each of my friends there is something that only some other friend can fully bring out." In other words, Lewis recognized the need for space between friends. He saw the need for multifaceted relationships that help us shine where another friend, even a close one, simply is not able. A friend who provides space relinquishes a possessive hold and helps us cultivate other friendships.

Another mark of the space–giving friend is a solemn respect for serenity. This kind of friend recognizes the value of a thoughtful silence and a private retreat. They know when to bite their tongue, and they know when to let you make your own path. Henry David Thoreau once said, "I never found the companion that was so companionable as solitude." Let's face it, there are times in everyone's life where we need to be alone. Times when we need to gather our wits and allow our soul to catch up. A good friend provides space for the companion of solitude to enter your relationship.

Of course, this same friend also knows when to return, when to break the silence and rejoin your journey. Even Thoreau, who certainly was fond of solitude, noted this lonely sentence in his journal, "It would give me such joy to know that a friend had come to see me, and yet that pleasure I seldom if ever experience." We need space for the companion of solitude, but even more we need a good friend. After all, this very space and separation provided by a friend draws us back to a full appreciation of our friendship.

A Good Friend Speaks the Truth

If we let our friend become cold and selfish and exacting without a remonstrance, we are no true friend.

—Harriet Beecher Stowe

"*Les, you sometimes drive yourself* so hard, pushing and pushing on an important project," someone recently told me, "that you sometimes place the same high expectations for driving hard on those around you, whether you know it or not." Ouch! Where did that come from? Talk about a zinger. Where did this guy get off telling me about how I treated other people?

Actually, he had every right to tell me what he thought. John was, and is, my friend. And he was

The sweetness of a man's friend gives delight by hearty counsel.

—Proverbs 27:9

right. I can focus in on a goal so intensely that I neglect other people's feelings in the process. We were starting a second helping of spicy chicken at our favorite Chinese restaurant when he gently lowered the boom. Truth is, John wasn't trying to berate or scold me; he was trying to save my neck. As a good friend, he didn't want me to get into a sticky situation with other members of a committee.

Good friends are like that. They speak the truth. Honesty is a prerequisite to their relationship. "Genuine friendship cannot exist where one of the parties is unwilling to hear the truth," says Cicero, "and the other is equally indisposed to speak it."

As painful as the truth might be, good friends are obligated to speak it. Now, this does not mean friends have license to insult, offend and badger. The Bible talks about speaking the truth in love (Ephesians 4:15) and that's the goal of an honest friend. The question is how does a friend do this? The answer involves a lot of respect. Without respect, honesty is a lethal weapon. Perhaps that's what caused Cicero to add, "Remove respect from friendship and you have taken away the most splendid ornament it possesses."

Good friends deserve the respect of knowing the truth. They deserve to know if they are hurting someone's feelings, being too aggressive, too lazy, too anything. If a friend cannot hear the truth from another friend the relationship suffers and so does that friend.

Some time ago I (Leslie) was counseling a twenty-something student named Lisa who came to my office in hopes of resolving a problem with a close friend. Lisa wasted no time in telling me the problem concerned her friend's stinginess.

"Jenny is so tight, she squeaks when she walks," Lisa confessed.

"Is this a new problem?" I asked.

"Oh no, it's been going on for years, but it's really wearing thin and I find myself wanting to avoid being with Jenny whenever money is involved."

Lisa went on to tell me how meticulous Jenny can be when trying to figure out a shared bill at a restaurant. She told me about the time it took an extra ten minutes to pay for parking at a down town garage because she wanted to make change for splitting the bill.

"How does Jenny respond when you talk to her about being so stingy?"

"Talk to her?!" she exclaimed. "I've never brought the subject up. I don't want to hurt her feelings."

Lisa and I spent the next several minutes exploring how much she valued her relationship with Jenny. Turns out, they were "best friends." But here she was, on the brink of tossing away an eight-year friendship because she didn't want to hurt Jenny's feelings. In other words, the one friendship she cared more about than any other was about to go under because she couldn't speak the truth.

> Be courteous to all, but intimate with few, and let those few be well tried before you give them your confidence. True friendship is a plant of slow growth, and must undergo and withstand the shocks of adversity before it is entitled to the appellation.
>
> —George Washington

With a little advice and coaching, Lisa mustered up the courage to confront Jenny on this annoying trait, and the problem began to slowly correct itself. The point to be learned here, however, is that friends who do not care enough to confront may save themselves a little awkwardness in the present, but they will end up losing their friendships in the future. Good friends deserve our honesty.

Honesty, by the way, is not only expressed in words; it also means being authentic as a friend. Have you ever known people who become fast friends because they have so much in common? It's amazing. Their work. Their wardrobes. Their tastes. Their backgrounds. Everything seems to be in sync. Almost over night, the two become like

You can trust a friend who corrects you.

—Proverbs 27:6 (CEV)

twins who can finish each other's sentences. That's when the red flag should go up. Why? Because the relationship isn't real. It's a pseudofriendship with the depth of a puddle. One or both of them is so eager to have a kindred sprit that they falsify themselves to get along. The relationship becomes what Emerson called "a mush of concession" with both parties impressing each other with how much they are alike.

True friends, the ones with depth that transcends the surface and meaning that connects the souls, aren't afraid to be honest and they aren't afraid to be themselves. True friends follow Emerson's advice: "Better be a nettle in the side of your friend than his echo." Translation: Speak the truth, because if you are afraid of making enemies you'll never have good friends.

A Good Friend Forgives Faults

Your friend is the person who knows all about you, and still likes you.

—Elbert Hubbard

Kevin is one of my best buddies. We met our freshman year in college and have been good friends ever since. But here I was, asking Kevin for his forgiveness. I hadn't committed a shocking betrayal or stabbed him in the back, but I had broken a promise that was important to both of us. And it hurt—him more than me. Sure, I had my reasons. At the time, at least, I thought they were pretty good. Looking back now, some ten years later, I'm not so sure. That doesn't really matter anymore, however. Kevin and I haven't talked about my broken promise for nearly a decade. Why? Because Kevin forgave me. It wasn't a flippant or sudden contrived act of forgiveness. He did some soul-searching, I'm sure. We had our share of uneasy distance. But somewhere back there, Kevin released the pain I caused and decided to remain my friend.

What a gift! Kevin, as I said, is one of my best buddies. I'd do just about anything for him, and he'd do the same for me. We're good friends, because of forgiveness. You see, when I didn't keep my word, Kevin had every reason he needed to decide that our friendship wasn't worth the effort. I'd let him down, big time. He was justified in calling it quits if he wanted. He could have said: "That's enough of Les Parrott. I don't need to waste my time cultivating a relationship with someone who doesn't deserve it." But instead, Kevin set his grievance aside and granted my wish. He forgave my failing.

Good friends do that. Their survival, in fact, depends upon it. Every friend we'll ever have will eventually disappoint us. Our friends aren't saints; they are ordinary people. Decent, yes. But even decent people hurt each other, sometimes deeply and unfairly. That's why a lasting friendship depends on forgiveness.

Do not use a hatchet to remove a fly from your friend's forehead.

—Chinese Proverb

Let's get this point clear right away: Not every offense of a friend requires forgiveness. Some slights need only be overlooked and forgotten. Too many good relationships fade because some snub—real or imagined—cancels out the friendship. Some people pout, brood, or blow up if their friends are not speedy enough in returning a phone call or if they are not included in a social event. They set such high standards for the relationship that they're constantly being disappointed. They can't let little things go; every minor lapse becomes a major offense. So they administer forgiveness like a general anesthetic until it numbs everyone to its original effect.

Treat your friends as you do your pictures, and place them in their best light.
—Jennie Jerome Churchill

Trigger–happy forgiveness is not forgiveness at all. Given out too quickly, too liberally, forgiveness becomes watered down. The quirks and cranks of our friend's annoying behaviors do not require forgiveness. Generosity? Yes. A sense of humor? Yes. Some tolerance? Yes. But not forgiveness. No. Forgiveness is reserved for a more serious mercy. Not for annoyances, but for the deeper wrongs friends do us.

There's another important point about forgiveness: When a good friend forgives another, it doesn't guarantee reconciliation. Forgiveness requires something of the offender as well as the offended if it is to restore the relationship. My former professor Lewis Smedes is one of the nation's leading experts on forgiveness. In his best-selling book, Forgive and Forget, he said something about what it takes to be reconciled after we forgive:

> You hold out your hand
>
> to someone who did you wrong,
>
> and you say: "Come on back,
>
> I want to be your friend again."
>
> But when they take your hand

and cross over the invisible wall

that their wrong and your pain

built between you,

they need to carry something with them

as the price of their ticket

to your second journey together . . . .

What must they bring?

They must bring truthfulness.

Without truthfulness, your reunion is humbug, your coming together is false.

Forgiveness will always heal the wounds in our memory, regardless of how a friend responds. But reconciliation requires that our friend own up to the truth of his or her fault and see the pain it caused. No masks or manipulation is allowed. If you forgive a friend for breaking a confidence and your friend denies it ever happened, the relationship will remain in limbo. There's no way around it. Reconciliation is a two-way street, requiring both grace and repentance. And good friends know it—whether they are on the giving or receiving side of forgiveness.

A Good Friend Remains Faithful

A faithful friend is a secure shelter;
whoever finds one has found a treasure.

—The Apocrypha

On August 9, 1974, after the house Judiciary
Committee had found that his actions during the
so-called "Watergate cover-up" offered sufficient
grounds for impeachment, Richard Nixon resigned
the office of the Presidency of the United States. And
it was at his lowest ebb in this scandal that Nixon
got a letter from Harold Macmillan, the former prime
minister of England. The letter read, in part, "I feel
impelled, in view of our long friendship, to send you
a message of sympathy and good will. I trust that
these clouds may soon roll away."

Years later, when Macmillan died, Richard Nixon wrote a tribute to him in The Times of London. Among the things he remembered about the prime minister was his letter of friendship. "What you learn when you fail," Nixon wrote, "is who your real friends are." So true. That's why we disdain fair-weather friends who support us only when it's politically savvy, easy or convenient to do so.

Harry Truman's secretary of state, Dean Acheson, must have understood this. He caused quite a stir

> *The typical expression of opening Friendship would be something like, 'What? You too? I thought I was the only one'—it is then that Friendship is born.*
>
> —C. S. Lewis

when he visited his friend Alger Hiss in prison. Hiss was a convicted traitor and it was bad politics to have any association with him. But when prudent politicians condemned Acheson publicly, Acheson simply said, "A friend does not forsake a friend just because he is in jail." Good friends don't desert you, even when you are in trouble. And they don't desert you, when it costs them something to remain your friend. Some call this faithfulness. Others call it loyalty or consistency. Whatever you call it, however, this trait is vital to your friendships.

Think about it. Everyone, at some time or another, enters a dark day and walks as one who has the plague—solitary, alone. We all experience our own private Gethsemane. And in this desperate time we discover who among our friends is faithful, if any at all. Those who come up empty handed in their darkest hour, take comfort in the saying: A dog is man's best friend. And they may be right, if no one emerges to make their road less lonely. But it is far better to travel with a companion who brings the human quality of life to another proverbial saying: A friend in need is a friend indeed. This is the mark of a good friend—they help you out when you're in trouble.

Faithfulness is the bedrock of any committed friendship. It gives the relationship a toughness to survive. That's probably why it seems so much more horrible that Jesus was betrayed by a friend than if a stranger hand turned him in. So much more monstrous that Caesar was stabbed in the back by his friend Brutus than had he been killed by Cassius, whom Caesar did not trust anyway.

While dark days reveal and separate our fair-weather friends from the faithful, it doesn't always take a scandal or a catastrophe to bring our good friends to light. We learn which friends stick with us in the daily routine of being ourselves. We note whether or not they keep a promise. Whether they gossip behind our back. A good friend knows our heart and likes us anyway. That's the very essence of faithfulness. Tell the truth: Don't you wonder if a friend will stop liking you when you feel unlikable? We all do. James Kavanaugh's poem cuts to the heart of our doubts:

Will you be my friend?

There are so many reasons why you never should:

Often I'm too serious, seldom predictably
the same,

Sometimes cold and distant, probably I'll
always change.

I bluster and brag, seek attention like a child,

I brood and pout, my anger can be wild . . . .

And if at times I show my trembling side,

I wonder, will you be my friend?

It's a wonder any friendships survive, really. Each of us brings so many problems and idiosyncrasies to a relationship to justify its dissolution. But that very fact is what makes faithfulness so valuable. That very fact is what has caused people down through the ages to seek a friend who sticks closer than a brother.

In the fourth century B.C., two Syracusan friends, Damon and Pythias, found themselves in a dreadful

Friendship is a sovereign antidote against all calamities.

—Seneca

predicament. Pythias was condemned to death by the tyrant Dionysius. Knowing his friend's need to put his house in order, Damon offered to temporarily stand in place for Pythias. Dionysius agreed to the arrangement but made it clear that Damon would be killed if Pythias did not return. As promised, Pythias did return to his own execution but he was met with a surprise. The tyrant Dionysius was so moved by the faithfulness of these two friends that he freed them both—and asked to be their friend.

CHAPTER 8

A Good Friend Laughs Easily

Friendship redoubleth joys, and cutteth griefs in half.

—Francis Bacon

It all started when we first met in grade school. A slight inflection. A knowing glance. Or a subtle gesture. The tiniest of things could make Greg and me laugh. We could bust up over anything and everything. On countless occasions—at church, around the dinner table, at school—we unsuccessfully tried to swallow our laughter to prevent embarrassment. We had the same funny bone and couldn't keep from using it. No wonder we're still friends.

Laughter does that. Any good friend will tell you that laughter is the shortest distance between two people.

In fact, what you find funny is a determining factor of whether or not you and another person will become and remain friends. Why? Because humor is always risky. What is appealing to some is appalling to others. In a survey of more than 14,000 Psychology Today readers who rated thirty jokes, the findings were unequivocal. "Every single joke," it was reported, "had a substantial number of fans who rated it 'very funny,' while another group dismissed it as 'not at all funny.'" Apparently, our funny bones are located in different places. Some laugh uproariously at the slapstick of Larry, Mo, and Curly, while others enjoy the more cerebral humor of Woody Allen.

I'll admit that my best friends—the ones who probably would take a bullet for me—don't think twice about busting me in the chops every now and then in the name of good-natured ridicule. And it always makes me laugh. Sitting around a table at a late night dive after a basketball game, for example, one of them might crack: "We were all impressed by that spineless prayer you call a jump shot." Which brings about the inevitable retort: "Yea, it's about as good as that serious medical disorder you call a golf swing." Leslie thinks this is more of a "guy thing." Maybe she's right. All I know is that some best buddies would never bond without a little needless needling. Think about Huck and Tom on the river, Butch and Sundance on the range, Hope and Crosby on the road. All of them made a friendship of joking around and became better friends because of it. Now, some people say this is a pathetic way to show affection. Maybe so, but try telling that to a small group of smart-aleck buddies sitting inside a cozy, satiric circle.

Of course, this isn't my primary mode of connection with my good friends. Truth is, we can be as tender as we are tough. The point is that when it comes to humor, it takes all kinds. That's what makes sharing a laugh with another person so special—and so risky. Humor is like a litmus test for mutual understanding between two people. Sometimes it fails miserably, but it also can reveal the possibility of a new connection. Perhaps more importantly, laughter is the fuel that keeps good friendships going once they are born. It's what enables friends to help each other cope in the midst of crisis. After all, where would we be without someone who could make us laugh?

Consider Janet, a young attorney, who wanted to impress her potential partners with an elaborate dinner. She and her friend Alison cooked all day and then Alison, in a traditional uniform, served the meal. All went well until the main course. As the Alison was bringing in the crown roast, the kitchen door hit her from behind and the platter flew across the room. Janet froze, regained her composure, then commanded, "Dear, don't just stand there. Pick up the roast, go in the kitchen, and get the other one!"

Eve Arden, the actress who portrayed Miss Brooks on popular 1950s television show by the same name, dealt with a practical joke that was sprung on her the closing night of one of her stage performances. Arden's costar and friend had the soundman ring the prop telephone in the middle of her monologue at a time not specified in the script. When the phone rang, Arden picked it up, paused, and then handed it to her leading man. "It's for you," she said.

So long as we are loved by others I should say that we are almost indispensable; and no man is useless while he has a friend.
—Robert Louis Stevenson

Humor helps us cope—not just with the trivial but even with the tragic. Psychoanalyst Martin Grotjahn, author of Beyond Laughter, notes that "to have a sense of humor is to have an understanding of human suffering." Charlie Chaplin could have said the same thing. Chaplin grew up in the poorest section of London. His mother suffered from serious mental illness and his father died of alcoholism when Charlie was just five. Laughter was Chaplin's tool for coping with life's losses. Eating a boiled leather shoe for dinner in his classic film Gold Rush is more than a humorous scene. It is an act of human triumph, a monument to the coping power of humor.

One does not need to be a professional comedian, however, to benefit from comedy. Victor Frankel is another example of how humor can empower a person to contend with horrendous circumstances. In Frankel's classic book Man's Search for Meaning, he speaks of using humor to survive imprisonment during World War II. Frankel and another inmate would invent at least one amusing story daily to help them cope with their horrors.

"If you can find humor in anything," according to Bill Cosby, "you can survive it." Researchers agree. Studies reveal that individuals who have a strong sense of humor—who can laugh easily with at least one other person—are less likely to experience depression and other forms of mood disturbance.

Scientists hypothesize that humor helps us cope because it offers a fresh perspective. When naturalist William Beebe used to visit his friend President Theodore Roosevelt at Sagamore Hill, both would take an evening stroll after dinner. Then one or the other would go through a customary ritual. He would look up at the stars, saying, "That is the spiral galaxy of Andromeda. It is as large as our Milky Way. It is one of a hundred million galaxies. It is 750,000 light-years away. It consists of one hundred billion suns, each larger than our sun." Then silence followed. Finally, one of them would say, "Now I think our problems seem small enough."

Every good friend knows that humor lends a fresh eye to our troubles and gives us a new perspective.

A Good Friend
Celebrates
Success

Most people enjoy the inferiority of their best friends.

—Lord Chesterfield

She came to my house every day, bearing freshly squeezed orange juice, pots of chicken soup, and loads of advice. My friend Kelly (not her real name) was a godsend, there for me at a horrible time when I (Leslie) was going through a tough spot at work and trying to pick up the pieces of my parents' divorce. I'd weep, and she'd put her arm around my shoulder, bucking me up and reassuring me that I would begin feeling better soon. When things didn't improve, she'd come over, listen to my new tale of woe, and tell me my limitless talents would soon take me out of despair.

Kelly was as solid as a friend could be—until I made a career transition and my life began looking up. Then, this woman who had been on the scene in my darkest days seemed to suddenly vanish. My phone calls to her went unanswered, and when I finally did reach her, there was coldness in her voice instead of enthusiasm at my good fortune. I

The deepest principle in human nature is the craving for appreciation.

—William James

agonized: What had I done to drive her away? I missed her, but she didn't seem to miss me. I felt like I had been dumped. And indeed I had. From her point of view, with my crisis over, there was no place for our friendship to go except out the window.

Certainly, a defining trait of a good friend is the

ability to stick with us in bad times. No one argues that. But sometimes we discover, painfully, that the true test of a friend's staying power is her ability to be supportive when things are going well.

Kelly, it turned out, was a perfect example of a foul-weather friend, someone who thrives during your disasters but becomes scarce when things improve. This kind of friend works to ferret out your troubles and even creates some you didn't know you had. But when the troubles don't exist, neither does she. Why? Because her role as a friend—or more accurately, as a "crutch"—is threatened when circumstances change. If you aren't needy, so the reasoning goes, you may not need her. So she wants to keep you in a needy state and finds it impossible to hang around if you're not.

A good friend, on the other hand, does quite the opposite. She celebrates your success. She spreads the good news and is happy for your achievement. Of all the traits a good friend possesses, in fact, this one may be the most telling. And the most challenging.

After all, almost anyone can befriend someone who is down on their luck. At some level, it makes us feel better about ourselves when we aren't the ones in anguish. By comparison, we think, we're doing pretty well. But when your best buddy hits a windfall? Gets engaged? Gets a promotion? A pay raise? Some notoriety? That can try even the most committed of friends.

So what's a good friend to do? The answer is probably not what you want to hear. It involves taking a wide-eyed look at the parts of yourself you wish didn't exist. It involves scrutinizing your jealous, suspicious, cynical, resentful, and competitive side. It means owning up to the fact that you may like serving as your friend's lifeguard more than as a cheerleader. Sure, it's an ugly side, but it's better to own up to it than allow it to keep you from being the kind of friend you want to be. In fact, if you don't come to terms with how you really feel about your friend's good fortune, you'll never be able to genuinely enjoy it. What's worse, your friend will know it.

Former therapist Carmen Renee Berry, who wrote *Girlfriends: Invisible Bonds, Enduring Ties* with Tamara Traeder, believes celebrating a friend's success can be especially difficult for women. She says most women don't know how to manage their competitive or envious feelings with friends because we have never had a chance to learn. "We weren't raised to beat our friends in games like men were," she notes. "We always

Man lives more by affirmation than by bread.
—Victor Hugo

did things together, and usually the activities weren't competitive. It takes a lot of courage for a woman to acknowledge her competitive feelings; but if she doesn't they will become an unconscious barrier, and they will not help the friendship."

Male or female, there is always potential for an unconscious barrier to keep you from celebrating your friend's success. We're tempted to bring friends down to earth when they're flying high. And we do it in the pious name of not wanting them to have a "big head." We become the ego police and wrangle their self-esteem in order to inflate our own.

I (Les) was recently giving a series of lectures in Australia when I discovered a fascinating phenomenon I'd never heard of before. It's called the "tall poppy syndrome." Over the years, it has become such a part of the Australian culture, so ingrained, I couldn't find anyone who could tell me its origin. But everyone knew the experience and how it worked. In Australia, if one person begins to succeed, if he grows taller than all the rest, it's up to his chums to cut him down to size. They cheer on the underdog, never the top dog. I suppose we have the same thing in the United States, to one degree or another. On my own university campus we call it "egalitarianism," because no one, in the academic's ideal world, should win any special favors.

Promotions are calculated and dispensed on a strict schedule once someone meets the demands of predefined criteria. Unlike the world of business, there's no wiggle room or fast track for special cases; we all must fit the same mold, or at least pretend to. But in Australia I was surprised to discover that an entire culture, not just a college campus, could be concerned with cutting down people who pull away from the pack.

I can't speak first hand about the state of friendships in Australia, but I can tell you that anyone who practices the tall poppy syndrome with their friend is missing out on a great deal of joy. Nothing takes the wind out of the sails of friendship more than wondering why your friend doesn't recognize your accomplishments. After all, good friends—a real friends—not only lend a hand when you're in need, they applaud your success and cheer you on when you prosper.

CHAPTER 10

A Good Friend Says a Prayer

God does nothing but in answer to prayer.
—John Wesley

From his childhood, Albrecht Durer wanted to
paint. When he was old enough, he left home to
study the great art and artists of the world. Along the
way, Albrecht became friends with a fellow student
who shared his passion for art. The two beginners
found it difficult to make a living and study art at
the same time, so Albrecht's friend offered a tremen-
dous sacrifice—he would work while Albrecht studied.
The idea was the once Albrecht's paintings began to
sell, his friend would then have his chance.

At first, Albrecht resisted his friend's offer, but

after much persuasion, he agreed. Albrecht worked faithfully as an artist while his friend toiled long hours to make a living.

The day came when Albrecht sold a woodcarving and his friend returned to his first love. As he began to paint once again, he made a dreadful discovery: the hard labor he had done had stiffened and twisted his fingers. He could no longer paint with skill.

Albrecht was filled with deep sorrow when he learned what had happened to his friend. One day as he was returning home unexpectedly, he heard the voice of his friend praying quietly for him, with his gnarled, toilworn hands folded before him.

from Lemonade

None goes his way alone: All that we send into the lives of others comes back into our own.

—Edwin Markham

Lemonade in the Desert

It was that image that inspired Albrecht to paint something that has since become world famous. "I can never give back to my friend the artistic skill he sacrificed for me," said Albrecht, "but I can show him how much I appreciate what he did for me by painting his hands, folded in prayer."

Albrecht Durer's inspired painting is recognized today by millions around the world who are blessed by the image of the classic clasped hands. And friends who know the story behind the painting are doubly blessed by the message.

"Prayer—secret, fervent, believing prayer—lies at the root of all personal godliness," wrote William Carey. When we pray God slowly and graciously reveals to us our blind spots, the parts of ourselves we need to change. Prayer is the catalyst for a new look at an old relationship. It causes us to see our friendships from God's point of view.

How does praying for a friend begin? It begins, according to renowned prayer expert Richard Foster, by attuning ourselves to "divine breathings." Listening to God is the necessary prelude to intercession. Once we hear the will of God we can then begin to pray it into our own life—as well as the life of a friend. Soren Kierkegaard once observed: "A man prayed, and at first he thought that prayer was talking. But he became more and more quiet until in the end he realized that prayer is listening."

So how does one know if he is listening to God? When there is a compulsion of compassion to intercede. This inner welling up of concern and kindness is a sure sign of fervent prayer. When you sense a strong compassion for a friend, it is a clear indication that you are being called to prayer for him or her. After all, when you genuinely love a friend, you desire far more for them than it is within your power to give, and that longing will cause you to pray. And if you are filled with compassion for your friend you eventually will know what to pray for.

If we are honest, there are plenty of times when we do not feel like praying for a friend. But prayer is like any other discipline, says Richard Foster. We might not feel like practicing the piano, but once we play for a while we feel like doing it. In the same way, our prayer muscles need to be limbered up. And once the blood-flow of intercession begins, we will find that we praying for a friend is as natural and simple as calling them on the phone.

So what does all this talk of prayer have to do with being a good friend? Here's our answer:

• Prayer enables us to make time for a friend when the urgency of life is keeping us apart.

• Prayer enables us to keep a confidence when we are tempted to let the secret slip.

A friend may well be reckoned the masterpiece of Nature.

—Ralph Waldo Emerson

• Prayer enables us to speak the truth to a friend when it would be easier to pretend it didn't need to be said.

• Prayer enables us to forgive a friend's faults by surrendering our right to hurt back just to even the scale of justice.

• Prayer enables us to remain faithful to a friend, even when we could find plenty of reasons to let the friendship fade.

• Prayer enables us to laugh more easily with a friend by seeing the funny side of life.

• Prayer enables us to celebrate a friend's success with a genuine spirit of gladness.

The bottom line? Prayer enables us to be a good friend.

A Prayer for My Friend

Epilogue

The Scottish philosopher David Hume said in 1740, "The difficulty is not so great to die for a friend, as it is to find a friend worth dying for." That's a catchy saying, but we think David Hume had it backwards. The real difficulty in finding a good friend is trying to be the kind of friend we want to find. Too often we look for a good friend before we work on being a good friend. Dale Carnegie, friendship guru and author of the mega-best-seller *How to Win Friends and Influence People*, said "You can make more friends in two months by becoming interested in other people than you can in two years by trying to get people interested in you."

Our prayer is that you might enjoy the company of a good friend. But remember: "Greater love has no one than this, than to lay down one's life for his friends" (John 15:13).

About the Authors

Drs. Les and Leslie Parrott are codirectors of the Center for Relationship Development on the campus of Seattle Pacific University (SPU), a groundbreaking program dedicated to teaching the basics of good relationships. Les is a professor of clinical psychology at SPU, and Leslie is a marriage and family therapist at SPU. The Parrotts are authors of the Gold Medallion Award–winning *Saving Your Marriage Before It Starts*, *Becoming Soul Mates*, and *When Bad Things Happen To Good Marriages*. They have been featured in the *New York Times* and *USA Today*, and have appeared on *CNN*, *CBS This Morning*, *NBC Nightly News with Tom Brokaw*, and *Oprah*.

To learn more about the Parrotts' resources and their national speaking schedule, please visit www.RealRelationships.com.

Resources by Les and Leslie Parrott

Pillow Talk
The Love List
When Bad Things Happen To Good Marriages
Relationships
Becoming Soul Mates
Proverbs for Couples
Love Is
Getting Ready for the Wedding
The Marriage Mentor Manual
Questions Couples Ask
Saving Your Marriage Before It Starts
Saving Your Second Marriage Before It Starts

Books by Les Parrott III

High-Maintenance Relationships
The Control Freak
Shoulda, Coulda, Woulda
Helping Your Struggling Teenager
7 Secrets of a Healthy Dating Relationship
Once Upon a Family
The Life You Want Your Kids to Live

Books by Leslie Parrott

If You Ever Needed Friends, It's Now
Marshmallow Clouds
God Made You Nose to Toes

196. HIGH STREET.

LEMONADE.

MIKE

GOLDEN

PETERS

LEMONAD

VENTURA COUNTY
Lemons

MOONBEAM

LEMONADE
LEMONS

PANAMA

SUMMERLAND

SAN MARCOS

SHAMROC